DREAM
KITCHEN

PREVIOUS WINNERS OF THE VASSAR MILLER PRIZE
IN POETRY

Scott Cairns, Founding Editor
John Poch, Series Editor

DREAM KITCHEN

OWEN McLEOD

WINNER 2018 VASSAR MILLER PRIZE IN POETRY

University of North Texas Press, Denton, Texas

10 9 8 7 6 5 4 3 2 1

Permissions:
University of North Texas Press
1155 Union Circle #311336
Denton, TX 76203-5017

The paper used in this book meets the minimum requirements of the American National Standard for Permanence of Paper for Printed Library Materials, z39.48.1984. Binding materials have been chosen for durability.

Library of Congress Cataloging-in-Publication Data

Names: McLeod, Owen, author.
Title: Dream kitchen / Owen McLeod.
Other titles: Vassar Miller prize in poetry series ; number 26.
Description: First. | Denton, Texas : University of North Texas Press, [2019] | Series: Number 26 in the Vassar Miller prize in poetry series | On Table of Contents page, [love] appears as a heart symbol.
Identifiers: LCCN 2018048166 | ISBN 9781574417494 (pbk. : alk. paper)
Subjects: | LCGFT: Poetry.
Classification: LCC PS3613.C5798 A6 2019 | DDC 811/.6--dc23
LC record available at https://lccn.loc.gov/2018048166

Dream Kitchen is Number 26 in the Vassar Miller Poetry Prize Series

The electronic edition of this book was made possible by the support of the Vick Family Foundation.

Cover and text design by Rose Design

CONTENTS

I

II

III

IV

V

VI

And I, then, tortured for old speech,
A white of wildly woven rings;
I, weeping in a calcined heart,
My hands such sharp, imagined things.

—Wallace Stevens

IN THE U-HAUL PARKING LOT

T-shirt armpits haloed with salt, Big Mac
on your breath, you wait for a cab to take you back
to the one-bedroom you just moved into.

Perched on a wire, crows daven and caw.
Styrofoam peanuts skitter across the lot, tumbleweeds
in this western. You're the stranger who rides a rental truck

into town, along with two cats for whom you feel
no affection, forced on you by the ex who called them
painful reminders, though their names are Squishy and Sam.

In a game she liked to play after sex, she was Squishy
and you were Sam, one cat cleaning the other's fur,
causing it to purr, yawn, and curl contented into a ball.

You'll forget about them, as you do with anything
you live with long enough. But you're not worried
about that right now. You're noticing the highway,

how the cars are just cans, how each can contains
a heart, how each heart—that soft and solitary pump—
throbs in a darkness never broken.

BEAM

You were too far under the truck
for me to reach you, the two of us stranded
in the middle of that dark rural road—

me confused, you quiet as usual, even
on the night I blurted out we were through.
I rolled you your little black flashlight.

I stood, then squatted, back against
the wheel—useless, it seemed. I needed
your forgiveness to fix the whole thing.

It came, somehow, though you didn't speak—
hands hard at work, torch clenched between teeth,
that light spilling out of your mouth.

STILL LIFE

The things I've done for you—
freed bats, frozen birds, scrubbed
brushes impossibly dirty,

hauled sacks of garbage
to the curb, clashed
with neighbors, turned thirty.

This isn't Carthage
to which we've come,
nor burning,

just a dinky town,
sad shops, stupid Buddhas,
seven months of cold.

I followed you—I your
hammer, you a moonlit desert,
no arms or legs, only doves,

you, the whom who loves
a headless doll, a Goodwill shirt,
painting drunk behind the door.

What do they mean anymore,
your cardinal barracudas
on scraps of salvaged board,

the imperial purple ceilings,
our candy cane floors,
these antique tapestries we can't afford?

We're burning after all,
our fifth fiery fall—
Ashes of a Lady with Parasol.

Remember when I used to sit for you?
Now I'm just a man who blows
the snow while dead.

No one knows
the outside of my head
or the inside of yours

like you do.

BLACK RING

Sadder than a long-gone summer's love song,
morning sun gives way to clouds, and they say
thunderstorms tonight. Tina's in the bathroom
crying to herself. I say lucky her. When I look
in the mirror, I see anything but me. Is it OK
to talk about my dreams? What about the one
in which a woman with wings descends the stairs
on the shoulders of a shit-faced satyr, and Tina
asks if we'll ever get a table at this place, and I say,
baby, we've done everything we can for our teeth?
How about the stuff that isn't a dream, the thing
that happened last night? I was out walking Otto
when I felt an insect crawling on my hand, which
I violently shook, thereby flinging my wedding ring
into the thistles and tall weeds that flourish along
the edge of the dog park. Do you know it's impossible
to find a black stainless steel band in thick vegetation
by the light of a dying iPhone while trying to rein in
a hyperactive Boxer-Doberman mix? Tina didn't.
She said why did I have to shake my hand so hard,
said I should have resized the ring two years ago,
said if I hadn't been so goddamn cheap we'd have
gold bands, said at least they'd be easier to see,
said that everything means something, said it's as if
I wanted to lose the ring. Then I said fine, fuck you
Dr. Freud, and I slammed the door on my way out
to spend the night on Wayne's floor. Which is why
this morning Tina is locked in the bathroom crying,
and why I'm back out here clawing through the piss-
soaked undergrowth like some sort of urban Gollum.
I read those books as a boy, but I didn't understand
how something so simple as a ring could contain

such power. Now I think maybe it's like Tina said:
Everything means something. Maybe some things
mean everything. A lady stops to ask if I need help.
I say I'm OK, and she asks me what I'm looking for.
This happens to be the exact moment when I find it.
I hold it out for her to see and say it used to be a ring.

IN MY WIFE'S VEGETABLE GARDEN

I was startled to find—among the beans
and cucumbers, the tomatoes and squash,
the peppers, eggplants, cabbage, and kale—
my head.

Or what seemed to be my head.
It was certainly a human head, pushing up
through the soil, taking root, the skullcap
sprouting hair, facial features developing:
weak chin, puffy cheeks, crooked nose,
lips too thin for kissing. Definitely me.

I casually brought it up. "The cucumbers
are coming along," I said. "I also noticed
a human head." "Oh, it's something new
I'm trying this year," she said. "Pretty sure
it won't work." I wanted her to say more,
but her tone made it clear the conversation
was over.

I didn't like where this was going.
I studied my head in the mirror. I worried
she wanted to replace it. I'll admit it's not
a perfect head, but then what's the point in
growing a duplicate? Would she harvest it
early, replace my old head with a younger
one? That would mean cutting off my head,
which is murder. Surely my wife is incapable
of that, I reasoned. But would it be murder?
Not if she were merely replacing a part.
Yet, how would that work? I hadn't heard
of any head transplants. Then again, I'd not
heard of heads growing in gardens either.

Next morning while she was jogging, I stole into the garden with a spade, intent on digging up my head and killing it. Have you ever tried to chop off your own head? It's not that easy, believe me, especially if it's staring right at you, helpless, up to its neck in dirt. I tried several times, but I just couldn't do it. I'd have to let it live. Maybe it would simply die on its own.

I discreetly monitored the growth of my head. By August, it was mature, complete with beard and glasses. My wife reaped tomatoes, beans, cucumbers, kale—but not my head. She tended to it with care, fed its mouth by hand, brushed its teeth, tousled its hair. I didn't know whether to feel jealous or touched. It'd been years since she'd shown such affection to me. We used to try to talk things through, fuck when we didn't want to, if only to be able to say we still did it. Now we slept in separate rooms, like siblings instead of lovers.

One night, I was wakened by the sound of soft laughter from the garden. I went to the window. In the moonlight, I saw my wife lying on her stomach, chin in hands, talking to my head as if to a college sweetheart. I wanted to know what she was saying to me, and what I was saying to her, but I couldn't make it out. I watched as they carried on, just the two of them, my wife and my head.

I was surprised, hours later, when she came to my bed. "You said such lovely things," she whispered, as she slid under the sheet. "Funny, too." "Remind me," I said, but she was asleep.

This continued through August
into early fall—my wife coming to me at night
after talking to my head in the garden. We made
love. I didn't speak, fearing my words wouldn't
compare to whatever I'd been saying out there.

Late October brought a killing frost. My head
was dead, frozen like a pumpkin in the snow.
My wife dug a hole and gently lowered me in.
When she came inside, fingers red and raw,
I asked if she'd try again. She didn't answer,
but silently took my head in her hands, waiting
for this skull to warm them.

COMPRESSED SPONGE

Grape-sized and neon green,
just add water and watch it swell

in the guestroom while she's away.
(God knows you need some fun.)

The sponge fattens into form. A heart? An angel?
A monster, it balloons to fill the room,

pins the door against the wall, bloats
into the hall and down the stairs, splinters

the family furniture and shatters
the windows as it grows.

You're banished to a cheap hotel
while glacially the green thing shrinks.

One day, after weeks on the phone,
she finally allows you back home.

You drag your bags upstairs,
but nothing is the same.

The guestroom bed is yours now,
the tiny sponge your pillow.

SOS PAD

We wake up in the wide ocean's middle,
barely afloat in our boat of burnt toast,
my head a black balloon, yours gone.
Not far, a cosmic drain swirls and roars.

In the red emergency kit, just a bunch
of old junk: hairball sonnets, left glove
language, a chunk of track from the sticks
and stones railroad, a bag of mummy rags

for bandages. I was going to be a whole
new dude; you, a transcendental dudette.
Those mountains there? They were so ours!
Now we're here, counting hammerheads.

Which did we first exhaust, the universal
or the particular? Either way, we shut up.
It's weird, don't you think, how the heart
becomes a gizzard for grinding bones?

Go ahead, fire your secret flares from the bow,
float your perfumed notes. Sternward, I'll craft
a one-man raft from your most expensive shoes.
Tomorrow, our children start to look like food.

ROCKET MAN

Death is at the door, the Reynolds Wrap
blade of her scythe slightly bent, her mom
on the sidewalk with a cup of warm beer.

I worry about things I shouldn't—
a pain in my knee, the stain on my shirt,
that puddle of oil underneath the car.

The trick is perspective, but it's tough
to view the world as if from outer space
while clinging to your love for what's in it.

Hours later, drunk, I step outside. Orion
hangs objectively above our dark house.
I recline in the yard and count down.

A jogger wakes me just before dawn,
fearing I might be a corpse. I tiptoe
up the stairs, hide out in my study.

When I finally descend, no one
seems to notice my pressurized suit
or the crater I made on re-entry.

My wife eats leftover candy from the bowl.
Our infant son teethes on a rubber skull.
The neighbors dismantle their graveyard.

Coffee's on the counter. I fill up my mug.
It's the cracked one that says *I Love You.*

MOTHER TONGUE

My wife speaks a tongue that isn't hers,
a language tone-deaf and atomic, full
of words like "barricade" and "moat."
Hers is wordless, as we understand words,
composed of pictures, brush-strokes, sounds—
sounds I still mangle after all these years.
In the middle of the night, when she can't sleep,
she slips downstairs to call her mother,
who still lives in the village of blue hills.
Sometimes I lie awake, straining to overhear
the sound of her voice, her true self speaking,
until she returns to our bedroom, a stranger.
She slides between the sheets, I rub her left hand,
and utter the words we pretend to understand.

GRIEF

You're eating haggis, of all things, except the stomach
is your son's. The stuffing isn't sheep's pluck,
but the heads of his G.I. Joes, wings
from model airplanes, a box kite, some drums,
a Nerf ball, comic books, trophies and balloons,
fish hooks and line, three pairs of small shoes.
At dawn, you sit down to this grotesque thing.
With blunted knife you shovel it in, trying to get
to the bitter end of it. Some days you do.
But next morning, there it is again—
whole, cold, new.

IGLOO

Barren fields, tin sky, clouds
the color of clouds. Why describe things
when things describe themselves?

Besides, there's nowhere to turn
when your shield against despair
becomes its source,

or when you hear
from the rear of the plane
your psychiatrist cry *Let's roll!*

I remember the day,
the sugar beach where waves
washed up an Igloo cooler—

red, white, totally barnacled.
My brother and I, we wondered
what was in it, something

wildly fragile we hoped
and, opening it, found air.
My self was in there, let loose

before I could know it.
Some days my head's a hovercraft,
chimneys are lighthouses,

each door a Rothko portal,
the hospital vending machines
stocked with Sumerian gods.

But it never lasts. Saturday's
infinite garage gives way
to the stairwells of Sunday,

to Monday's dismal milk.
I rejoin the tribe, read labels
in the Safeway cereal aisle.

In February, the parking lot
is ringed with mounds of snow.
I narrow my eyes, imagine

the mounds as waves, and pray
for them to crest, to crash,
and bring in, sweetly, me.

SOMETHING YOU LEFT TO ME

This box of glass vials with black rubber stops.
A strip of brown tape runs the length of each vial.

Scribbled on each strip, the name of a national park:
Zion, Yosemite, Yellowstone, Redwood—

nine samples in all, but you wanted still more
before the thing in your lungs finally killed you.

The vials look empty, but I know they're not—
not because you told me, but because I was there.

Each contains air from the park on the label,
air the only stuff you could steal without guilt.

You'd hold the vial above your head and explain
how no one can die while surrounded by beauty.

Which is why it ended in a machine-filled room,
stifling, falsely lit, encircled by a plastic curtain.

Air was all you needed. I should have crawled in,
unstopped the vials, and touched each mouth to your lips.

ADELIA

People have tricks for falling asleep. Hers
is to imagine, room by room, every place
she's ever lived, beginning with the first
house she remembers—a small Victorian

in Sewanee, Tennessee, its buckled porch,
the peeling yellow turret. From there she moves
to Virginia, Alabama, Washington State,
North Dakota, Arizona, Massachusetts,

to a Brixton flat above the fish & chips,
a cabin in Sweden, a temple in Vietnam,
a tent on the beach of some Pacific island,
a concrete block in Mali, a discarded tire,

an Exxon bathroom, an oil drum, the moon,
this rehab clinic in the Ozark mountains.
If, by then, she still can't sleep, she returns
to Tennessee, to the abandoned cemetery

across the street. They dared her to climb
that crumbling angel, stare in its eyes for five minutes
without blinking. If you do it, they said, you'll die
on the spot. Tonight she means to prove it.

THE EIGHTEENTH HOLE

Once a year we visit this place, inhale
its vapors, stare at the silent shrubbery,
perform mental chores, delete junk mail.
What was it about you we miss, exactly?

Your amphibious wristwatch?
Your waffle house Buddhism?
The distinctive new-car smell of your scotch,
the rigors of your sand trap curriculum?

Memory's a dull pencil, for sure,
scorecards smeared by disputes beyond
all adjudication. Still, probably better
than dredging the country club pond

for lost balls. Thousands beneath
the surface, caked in mud, awaiting the day
of judgment. We lay a fresh wreath.
The green graves roll on like a fairway.

JAKE'S LADDER

No pills for eight days but this morning it's okay, the air
cool and damp, hills filled with the fresh black skeletons
of trees, Triceratops asleep behind me as I drive alongside
the river that flows like my terrible lizard's lust to the sea.
There are things I must remember: the blue and Bondo van
packed with second-hand stuffed animals, the loneliness
of the loser's campaign sign, the love I felt for everyone
at 7-Eleven, the face of each person whose hand I let go, how
we're all stumbling in our own way toward God. In the bed
of my pickup, Triceratops wakes and snuffles in the hay.
It knows the way by heart, smells the smoke of wet oak
drifting from my man's chimney, knows I've got the cash.
It's not too late to turn back, clean out the gutters, sweep
the porch, brew a pot of black coffee and read a magazine.
But we're here now, Triceratops whining and straining
at the leash, and Jacob from the top rung beckoning.

IN THE CAR ON THE WAY TO MY GIRLFRIEND'S BROTHER'S FUNERAL

I've been out of work for nearly two years.
None of my old clothes fit me anymore.
Still, she wants me to love the rosy streaks
of cloud we're headed toward. I do, sort of,
but mostly I'm studying the way debris
builds up on the shoulders—cigarette butts,
bits of glass and shredded tire, fast food bags,
condoms, possum bones, God knows what else,
like a trail of weird crumbs to Woodlawn.
She's crying now, so I don't mention that.
I say something nice about the pink clouds,
then flip down the visor to check myself out.
Her brother and I were about the same size.
I brush the dandruff from a dead man's suit.

FLOOD

The water where we horsed around
was once the sky above a rural town—
family farms bought up, cleared out,

drowned in the reservoir created
by a Depression-era dam. My brother
dove for traces, remains, surfaced

with pebbles, twigs, rotting leaves,
stuff that carpets the floor of any lake.
Then something strange, he said,

impossible to lift. I dove, expecting
an old stump, but felt instead a pair
of rusted metal rails running parallel

into the gloom on either side of me.
Was it forty years ago? Today, waiting
for a freight train to rumble through,

I thought I saw my brother peering
from a window of the school bus
up ahead of me. I rubbed my eyes

and he was gone—then the train,
the bus, the buildings too, the voice
on the radio calling for heavy rain.

THE SADDEST POEM IN PENNSYLVANIA

The summery part of summer long gone,
too late to unlock the secret of seeing things
in a new and startling way, too late to locate
my most honest innermost self, I'll have to go
with what I've got: two or three clichés, half
a case of the local microbrew, one-quarter tank
of Sunoco gas, and four ounces of personal lube.
Actually, it's not so bad being dead. The sun
hurts your eyes and nothing tastes like anything,
but apart from that it's pretty much the same
as being alive. Besides, not many people notice,
and those who do don't have the heart to tell you,
not even your shrink, who seems to think the trick
is white pills instead of pink. The hardest part
is that it's almost impossible to cry. I've tried it
in restroom stalls, art deco diner booths, and flat
on my back on that black marble ring around
the Lincoln Center fountain at three o'clock
in the morning. No luck. Last time it worked
was nearly six years ago. I was on my knees,
scrubbing streaks of melted chewing gum from
the dryer drum with a neon-pink dish sponge,
my upper body swallowed by the machine.
I must have stuck my head in the Whirlpool
a dozen times since then, but I can't recapture
that singular moment—the sensation of being
back in the womb, halfway through the breech,
weeping, hanging on, knowing what's to come.

RIVERS

The Delaware's a greenish black river here,
flanked by other, slower rivers—fields

of snow, rows of leafless sycamores larger
than God, two shoulderless snaking roads.

I'm in the truck on my way to buy a beast
from a man who slaughters the animals himself,

their blood a red river that flows into ours.
I write the butcher's check, tuck a pig

part by part into the bed, the heavy head
a gift for my Chinese friend's New Year.

She lives by the moon and I by the sun,
two rivers of time draining into one sea.

My papery hands grip the steering wheel
as I pass the bad sign, *Snyder's uneral H me*.

I get home, unload, break for coffee
and a roll, nap on a surplus Army cot.

I cough up a coin for Charon in my dream.
We slide into the river of meat.

CUMULUS MEDIOCRIS

Knowledge of having lived the wrong life
will not come through a crack in the sky,
a blinding beam of light, divine revelation
of what should have been. It will come,
if at all, in the form of something small—
running out of gas while mowing the lawn,
changing a tire on the highway in the rain,
lugging your dad's soiled mattress to the curb,
watching a spider on the waiting room wall.

You will not collapse or rend your clothes.
You will not wail or renounce the world.
You'll simply wait for the knowledge
to pass, like the shadow of a lone cloud,
cold and colossal, darkening the valley—
hushing the blackbirds, stunning the bees,
covering the ground on which you stand,
sweeping through you without a sound,
then crossing over the mountains to the sea.

TWELVE PZALMS TO OUR LORD BUBBA

#1

Oh Bubba, biggest ghost to rule the world,
give him yer attention. His bills are all past due
& flies fly in his room because no screens
& they have nothing to eat but he. It's not so bad
they said. He is not at war or sick or very dead.
Many be those who are he say & even him too
in a certain way (or ways). Bubba, look in his head
& tell him what is up with it. Many docs did shine
their lights & cut him many scrips. Grace & love
he's heard of but he fear he don't believe it.

#2

He went to school & learned the sums
but now he figures out no stuff. What is wrong
with this man? Sick, for sure, with everything
he is under them suns. (OK, not everything,
but enough.) He tried to read the Book, listened
hard to pulpit men sing. Trees & cars can he see
for sure, but to him not much does this look
like pasture tended by Bubba, or even a link
in a great chain o' being. He remembers the girl
from driver's ed & the flesh of hers he saw for real.
Now he has strange hairs & bad breath & his bod
is no longer good. Oh Bodiless Bubba, do you know
how it feels to be dying yet already dead?

#3

Fine he was & proud, feet kicked up in Sterling's
reading rooms, profound clouds floating from his
big fat brain. Then he fucked it all up. Found
nude & unconscious on Silliman quad,
he was dismissed. A while it took for the sinking
in. No respectable place would hire him
on a permanent basis. Nomadic he became,
inconsolably pissed, wandering the land,
Socratic method replaced by remedial tutoring
in whatever. Together who can hold
under such conditions a life? He, for one,
could not. Dear Bubba, he bores you again
(as he limps into the rusting sun).

#4

Once with friends with money on a boat
did sail he to the middle of a lake
& envied them a bit. (OK, a lot.)
Alone that night on deck a not-his-wife
crept up, his throat her lips did kiss & made him
ache for that sort of life. Hey Bubba, why can't
everyone be rich & if not everyone,
why not he? A cottage above a roaring sea
& soup & grilled cheese sandwich brought in
on a tray? Work he could get done that way
instead of, as it is, hauling papers in a plastic bag
to Franchise Café, giving no tips & bad grades
while the Bubba inside him withers & fades.

#5

His home? A hamlet in the heart of nowhere's
middle. What a dump. Downtown a redbrick ruin,
outskirts strips of malls & McD's. Where once were
cornfields, homes erupt in rows of Tyvek molars.
He can't escape. License revoked for the foreseeable
future, bus too sad & tickets too much, no trains
out of here but freight. There is a teensy airstrip,
sure, but only for local oral surgeons.
He rides his bike as if a boy from A to Z
& sweats. Bubba flies over him in jumbo jets
to cities of tremendous sparkle. He shouts
to Him *avast ahoy!* but Bubba don't even wave.

#6

He reads *King Lear*, hears Beethoven stringed
& late, spots a bird & believes Bubba abides,
dead leaves included. He feels good, fears no thing,
drinks wine to celebrate. Mostly though he wonders
if the bridge is high enough. No one knows but you
(& Drs. Gupta, Friedman, Craig) that generally
he wants to X himself & nearly did times two
plus once did stab hisself in the leg with scissors
in a Walmart bathroom. X is surely stuck on his list
of things to maybe do. He bores you with this boringness
he knows & is sorry too. Hevvin should send him
something soon, but Bubba forgot his address.

#7

The price of a driver's license? Once a week
in the Presby basement: "Mah name is Yukon Jack,
and I'm an alkeeholic." This message brought
to you by his sponsor, a patriotic man
of considerable patience & inveterate guzzler
of Diet Pepsi. Growed up 'round here, fork-lift
operator of consummate skill, twenty years sober
as a drill sergeant, set straight by the epilepsy
of his youngest daughter. He recounts the night
she nearly choked to death. Comatose at supper,
he could not perform the maneuver.
His ex-wife's the one who saved her.
Now we bow our heads, Higher Power invoked,
but not even a shrug from Bubba.

#8

Would you believe he has three kids?
Two by wife one, one by wife two, luckily
for everyone no wife three. He was with wives
quite busy in bed & not (he admits) just his.
For this forgive him, won't you Bubba?
He promised to change, together get his act,
frighten up & stray right. He writes his three
but does not mail a single letter. Loves
them all, though strange they are to him
& he to his pups. He is ashamed & no good
for them. If they saw his teeth & how he
fails to live, they'd cry. The girls he misses,
the little boy most, youngest of the three.
Bless them, Old Bubba, if only you could.

#9

He wakes to find two Cheetos in his beard.
Weird. He don't remember eating those.
Resolves to shave the hairs he's grown
(but rarely groomed) for close to twenty years.
The rub: no razor blades he got nor cream.
He saddles up & rides to CVS on foot,
rustles up the gear he needs plus a case of beer
to celebrate. Dude is all set, but his hands
do quiver. He quaffs a can & more to steady hisself.
In the glass, he stares doleful at this cowpoke
& the skunk around his neck, which he prepares
to cut. Forgive him, Bubba. He drunk.

#10

He left the water running in the sink,
which did overflow & flood the folks below.
Found on the floor, face down, seeming dead,
a case of empties in the tub, plus blood
& a kennel stink. Thing is, he did not try
to X himself. Last thing he recalls, he was
shearing off his fur. Next thing he knows,
yer friendly EMT man is peeling open
his eyes, while hisself is sprawled on the tiles,
hurt terrible in the head, which he did halve
on a cast iron radiator on the way down.
Now, dear Bubba, he sports a shavéd crown,
half a beard, & a whole unholy hospital bill.

#11

He gathers twigs & bark by the lake, builds fire
for the pot & in the dream (cont.) boils herbs for tea,
sits on a mossy rock & makes no mistake
his whole life pretty much. He wakes on a surplus
Army cot, scalp downy as a baby rat's,
scar pulsing, whiskers gone, much weakened
(inexplicably, for nothing has he had to eat
for three days now but Bars of Power). He is
good for nothing but TV, its trucks & pizzas
& polar bears ripping into ripe seal blubbah
to the voice of Sir David Attenborough.
Crying through tubes, the soul of the world!
Is anything sadder or lonelier, Bubba?

#12

Right outside his room: hammer of jack
& beep beep trucks & men in hats of yellow plastic.
Rubber cones ring a fresh crater in the street.
He grabs a stack of papers, locks cats in a room
with food & water, hikes to the landfill,
now a park. The sun is too hot! Insects shoo!
To Franchise Café he lugs his lot, wearily
& without joy, for he knows what awaits him there:
people & music he don't like listening to.
He camps at a corner table, nurses coffee
from a trademarked cup. Nearby a glitter-nailed
teenybopper cries. He suffers there till
the workday's up, then shoulders his load,
crawls back to the hole, climbs in &

CLICK HERE TO GET RIPPED

Play the lottery. Pray all you like.
Odds are, tomorrow you'll be stuck
in some basement washing socks.

Remember when we let Jesus
into our hearts? That lasted, what,
three months? Now we're on eBay,

selling industrial cornstarch
in jars labeled *Muscle Builder Max*.
Between shipments we smoke hash

with Randall the midnight janitor.
When stoned, he can't shut up about
making America great again.

What Randall doesn't understand
is that America is Jesus, that Jesus
isn't coming back, that when Jesus

leaves your heart he leaves it worse
than he found it—punched-in walls,
rooms crammed with fast food bags,

plumbing & electric shot to shit.
Meanwhile, millions of adolescent boys,
keenly sensing where the future's at,

set their sights on getting ripped.
Don't forget the heart's a muscle, lads.
We're here to help with that.

BODY IMAGE

She was barely nine when her brother
baked her Malibu Barbie in the oven.

Now forty, parked in the shoulder,
weeping for a fox pancaked and rotting

in the road, she recalls the melted head,
her perfect body puddled, then pried

from the cookie sheet with a metal spatula
and tossed in the trash without ceremony.

The world blurs. She reaches for her face
but finds Barbie's instead, her hair a mass

of spent filaments. Just then, up ahead,
a vehicle with flashing hazards pulls over.

A municipal worker exits the truck
and scrapes up the fox with a shovel.

SONNET FOR A CHANGED CLIMATE

From the balcony above the pool party we can see
the incoming asteroid. No biggie. We're happy
with the way things are, plus or minus a python.
We invested early in seawater, worshipped the sun
as it shrank the poles, purchased a fleet of surplus
Blackhawk helicopters, perfect for strafing refugees
who huddle along the rim of the Grand Canyon,
now filled to the brim with dead tennis balls.
There's room for nostalgia, romanticism even,
but don't kid yourselves about the way things were.
It's better to be an apocalypse hipster, surfing
the tubes of a haywire sea, than a dandruffy old man
recalling flecks of glitter in the mud. The prairie, for him,
was just a bunch of grass, but for us it's one huge engine.

SHOP-RITE

Triceratops doesn't like it here.
Morgue-bright, words that don't mean,
the people reading *People* magazine.

He shrinks to something small,
wheels his way to Produce, grabs
a bag of mixed greens, feels lust

for a mom in sweats. Brown hair
piled high, she coos to her tot, legs
dangling like sausages from the cart.

Triceratops recalls a prehistoric trip,
back when he was one of them and had
a mommy. She showed him the tank

of lobsters. Sullen heap, claws
cuffed by rubber bands, eyes black
unblinking beads. *They're alive*, she said.

Perhaps that's when it began—
the growth of horns, the bony frill,
his lips curling into a beak.

Millions of years on, nearly extinct,
he lumbers down the aisle, buys
a box of Jurassic Park Crunch.

Midnight finds him behind a bowl.
Marshmallow dinosaurs float to the top,
the milk gone pink with their blood.

MEMENTOMORI.COM

Lugging a corpse with you everywhere you went.
Strapped to your back.
Slumped in a wheelchair.
Dragged on a sled or pulled in a red wagon.
The corpse keeping you focused on your mortality.
Reminding you that ultimately you're just a corpse.

At first it was a fringe thing.
Hipsters only.
Then celebrities got involved.
Hauling their corpses to the Oscars and whatnot.
Corpses tumbling out of limos.
Corpses in Chanel gowns and Armani tuxedos.
Actors thanking their corpses in the speeches.

Eventually everyone was dragging around a corpse.
By then they'd stopped reminding us of death.
They'd become more of an accessory.
A status thing.
It was like, how heavy is your corpse?
Is it a local corpse?
Did it die naturally?

Corpses went way up in price.
Demand did too.
This inevitably led to a market in discount corpses.
Small brown bodies from unknown parts of the world.
You weren't too sure how they died.
They were much cheaper than big white corpses.
Not to mention a lot lighter.

But even discount corpses were too expensive for poor people.
Poor people had to make due with fake corpses.

Which were basically repurposed mannequins.
Poor people schlepping these mannequins around.

Then celebrities got into that too.
Ditching their corpses for mannequins.
You know, to show solidarity with poor people.
Soon everyone traded their corpses for mannequins.
Hauling mannequins behind them wherever they went.

Except the mannequins did not remind us of death.
They reminded us instead that really we're just mannequins.
Neither alive nor dead.
This turned out to be too unpleasant to think about.
Even more unpleasant than death.
No amount of accessorizing the mannequins seemed to help.
It just made things worse.

Slowly but surely people abandoned their mannequins.
First the celebrities, then everyone else.
No one ever went back to corpses.
We just returned to the way things were.
Doing the normal, everyday things.
Like going to funerals.
And malls.

HERE'S THE THING

We spot a silver greyhound, a red Pegasus,
three skulls, two horses, one red fox, a small tiger
with orange and black stripes, a large tiger
with blue and white stripes. We see lots
of other things along the way, mostly minor
variations on the theme. It's a long drive.
Finally we arrive, plop down on fat couches
in the shadow of inflatable Santa. We exchange
a bunch of gag gifts. Thanks for the plastic mallard,
which I'll use whenever actual mallards fail me.
I hope you enjoy the old tennis shoe, a vintage
Converse high top, which is in fact Lord Buddha.
It's the night of our lives. We remember the hymns,
but are unprepared for the reality of our togetherness.
Conversation turns awkwardly to TV, a battle
for the AFC, plus other emergency talking points.
Each of us, alone and as if on cue, seeks refuge
in darker, cooler rooms. In the morning, we inspect
the neighborhood, frown on a house built too close
to the lake. We help drag bags of trash to the curb,
aware of a yearning whose name we never utter.
Family pods form, drift toward the driveway.
Adults shake hands or clumsily hug. Kids crawl
into the bellies of vans and power up their screens.
Four hours later, we pass the weathered sign:
You are leaving Pennsylvania. Please come back!
Silence settles over the SUV. We pray
that what matters is how much we meant to love.

THE REPUBLIC

The world of The End is near: pale men
in blue suits replace redwoods with tree-sized
Burger King balloons, tile the valley of Yosemite
with Arctic Fresh gum, make a digital billboard
of the moon. Hey, do you remember waking up
in a white-cloaked wood, ill-equipped and numb,
the flap of our cheap-ass tent frozen shut?
I was content to sleep in and screw, but you,
who would not be denied the sunrise, thawed
the zipper with your breath and OMG the light!
Now we're at this Exxon, you in the passenger seat
scrolling through tweets, me watching gas pump TV.
I need you to say it'll be OK and mean not good
or bad but bittersweet, the way it seems to God
if there is a God. Even if there isn't, isn't the idea
almost enough? I know old Plato was big on ideas:
The Beautiful, The Good, The River, The Tree.
These days I pray there are such things, eternal
and pristine, like far away stars we can almost see
beyond the glare of the dead moon's messaging.
We'd wake up there in the ideal tent, unzip
the old skin, and fly, perfected, to The Sun.

LA FIN DE L'ÉTÉ

To everything luscious, to all things green
or pink, to everything purple or blue,
to rattling machines in every chilled room,
to fairgrounds littered with paper cups,
to each pair of lips she's ever known,
to planets, stars, and nebulae unknown,

she bids farewell in a language unknown
to all but her. If you could see her green,
see her grand, in her gilded glory known
best by those who love her—O, you'd be blue
by god, depressed deep down, drowning in cups
of clover honey. You'd rush to her room

in that temple above the town, the room
where she roils from a core unknown.
You'd roll in her meadow of buttercups,
her leaves viridescent, her tattoos green.
Begging her to stay, you'd pray to the blue
sky. You'd bloody your knees on the known

to hold her here, hold her hair, perfume known
throughout the town. Her light floods every room.
The charms of her bracelet are cornflower blue.
But in truth she is doomed. Up from unknown
comes scarlet blood; down goes all the green.
Bees drink the dregs from petaled cups.

At the river's edge, she kneels and cups
her hands. Swans sing to her, for they're known
to be her lovers. She drinks to her green
old age. In this—her season—there is room
for one more day, one more night of unknown
songs from the trees, one more moon of blue.

Meanwhile, glaciers calve bergs of weird blue
up north. Inuit warm their hands with cups
of Labrador tea. Above the clouds, unknown
currents run cold, then colder, until known
to us as snow. We walk from room to room,
battening the windows. Apples shed their green.

She curls up in her vaulted room, this white and blue
sphere, by her fading gown known to be soon unknown.
We toast to her green, then bury—sweet bulbs!—the cups.

TRICERATOPS ❤ YOU

The bottle says one but Triceratops
needs two to make the want to not be
not be. As if you care. As if sadness

were anything new. As if Triceratops
cares or even knows about you.
Well, surprise, surprise: *it do.*

What else can explain the way
Triceratops weeps when it watches
wall-mounted waiting room TV,

spots a queue of angry SUVs
in the Dunkin' Donuts drive-thru,
reads even one word of news.

Suck it up and deal? Toss dimes
in the kettle outside the mall? Hoist
a sign and join the march on DC?

Done, done, and done. Now what?
The surf's still way too up, nothing
from the Tower but dumbass tweets,

and Triceratops dying in the weeds.
If the good Laura Dern and Sam Neill
were here, they'd hug & kiss & care

for old 'tops, which is very sweet,
but not even Steven can save the island
from blowing up. Till then, remember:

Triceratops loves you because it knows
what extinction means. It means *not a thing.*
It means enjoy the ice cream.

LETHE

Two wood ducks work a dark eddy.
Lodged between rocks, the chopped-off head
of a parking meter.

Beneath the spume, brown trout root
for caddisfly cases. Snow starts. I straighten
to catch a few flakes on the tongue.

For fifty years I've been reading this book.
I mean to mark the page
before drowsing off, but every morning

I find it fallen to the floor, shut.
I don't remember where I was,
who was who, or how the story goes.

And so every morning, each time
with more trouble than the time before,
I bend to the floor, pick up the book,

and begin the reading again.

NORTHEAST KINGDOM

Like ashes, like prayer, like flowers are my physics.
My life is the length of the lake in this, the season
of fire and mist, of children with sharpened sticks,
of camouflaged men in the wooded hills, of deer
brought down then laid to rest according to the laws
of meat and steel in the beds of rusted-out Rams.

I've studied the meteorology of these rooms, tracked
the black rectangles and the flaming boats that float
above her body as she sleeps. She paints her portion
of the world as if her skull were a fractured window.
When I come down for coffee and bread, she says
she dreamt me as a bear with a buck's antlered head.

The lake's edge is laced with ice. Our geology is glass,
the granite ground into powder from which this cup
was formed. Please understand: I do not understand
the nature of things. The objects of my thought are not
objects themselves, but the modes through which
I think them, the geography and chemistry of paint.

Anything can represent anything else, but we resist
the idea that things signify themselves, that the rocks
along the shore are names. I find a palm-sized flat one,
fling it, watch it skip across the surface before it sinks.
I rub my antlers against a birch, claw the papery bark.
Velvet means that I was here—marks, that I am me.

THONG MAN

You've rubbed your sticks together for umpteen years
and still no balloon animals. What's the secret
to the secret of happiness? That guy over there, he swears
it's a sea of thongs. You've never placed very much stock
in such systems, preferring instead evening classes once a week,
solitary mornings in the county herbarium, bumming
the occasional cigarette. It's all good, pretty much,
until it isn't. That's when you begin to wonder
whether thong man isn't on to something after all.
He never seems vexed by the eternal questions:
What are the roots that clutch? Which roads diverged
in a yellow wood? How could a rabbit be king of the ghosts?
You can't Google the answers, so don't even try. The most
you'll discover is your old college girlfriend, the one
you thought was crazy, is now a veterinarian in Cleveland.
Meanwhile that man perfects his tan, lounges Buddha-like
in a cabana chair, employing your paperbacks as coasters.
Why not join him for a while, order an umbrella drink?
He'll remind you that the sun is Apollo, god of poetry,
master of metamorphosis. Then he'll playfully nudge
your ribs and grin—at you, in your tangerine thong.

SOMEONE JUST SEARCHED FOR YOU

What did they find? That photograph of me
from 1998? My CV, updated seven years ago?
Maybe the Twitter account I opened in 2012,
the one with zero followers, no tweets, and me
depicted by the default icon: nondescript egg
against a baby blue field, suggesting something
unborn, unrealized, not yet ready for the world.
Whatever they found, it wasn't me. Strange,
since I'm not hiding anywhere. I'm right here
at Supercuts, across the street from Applebee's,
watching a toddler fumble with the house
he fished from the second-hand toys stashed
in a laundry basket near the door. The house
opens on a hinge, a Fisher-Price diptych,
revealing rooms of grimy yellow plastic.
Still can't find me? I'm inside the house,
seated at the miniature piano. I stumble
over a sonata, then stop and stare dumbly
at the keys. I remember a box of old letters
in the attic, too poignant to read, too precious
to burn. I remember cave paintings, amulets
of bone, dead leaves eddying on the back porch,
my failure to capture the *thisness* of things.
I open the piano lid and crawl inside.
If they search long enough, they'll find me.

CROSSING THE WATER

Her sonnet is a sheet of rice paper,
folded until a miniature boat
rises from the waves of her hands.
She glides to the frosted window.
A red-tailed hawk floats above the river,
then plummets in a bolt of rust.

These turnip-white skies and fields of rust
are not her home. She studies the paper
for news of it, surveys the cold river
for signs, unfolds and refolds the boat.
In her language, the word for window
also means mirror. She puts her hands

to the glass, reflecting her mother's hands.
On the outskirts, abandoned rails rust
in the weeds. Once, through the window
of a long-ago train, she released a paper
crane, praying it might fly to the boat
from which her father worked the river.

He wouldn't have understood this river,
its origin or end, the gnarled hands
that claw the bottom of the boat,
its twice-a-year torrent of rust-
colored water. She folds a paper
crane and tapes it to the window.

It's a strange mirror, this window,
distorting what's behind her—the river
she once knew, the crane made of paper,
the house built by her father's rough hands
now reflected as a barn of rot and rust,
his vessel shrunk down to a tiny boat.

Today she asked them about a black boat,
a black lake. Her students stared out the window—
the silence of astounded souls, or rust
gathering on the oarlocks? The river,
for them, is just a bunch of water, hands
hands, the poem a piece of paper.

Her tea tastes of rust. Her breath fogs the window.
The ghost of her father's boat drifts down the river.
In his nest of cupped hands, the crane of folded paper.

REPORT FROM THE SURFACE

Day 17531 on Station No. 3, bitterly
cold, no civilization in sight, perpetual
night beyond the ragged dome.

Volcanoes in the distance. I paint
one now. Perhaps that's why I'm here.
I leaf through old logbooks for clues.

Everything I've felt seems measurable
in standard units. Plants and animals arrive
in waves, disappear, predictable

tides of petals, feathers, fur.
I squeeze breakfast from a tube,
check the traps, tap the rocks.

Beneath every language is another
set of signs, each a layer of sediment
varying only in color, density,

and fossilized ephemera.
There's no ghost in the machine.
It's machines all the way down.

Still, I map the stars, the stations
of the sun. I test the air for ash.
Which is observation, which is art?

I'm not happy with my volcano.
Too loyal to the way it is; not true
enough to the way it seems.

My reports go out as coded transmissions.
I can't tell whether they're ever received.
I've not heard anything in all these years.

For all I know, today is Christmas Day.
Merry Christmas to all, if that's what it is.
Tonight I'll decorate a dying tree.

DREAM KITCHEN

Each thing, ultimately,
is three connected things.

The earth, for example,
is sky, rock, and sea.

The Trinity, for some,
is another instance.

Yet always overlooked
is your dream kitchen.

One part is in a penthouse
with a view of Central Park.

You've never been there,
but can almost imagine it—

granite countertops, an island
the size of Malta, vintage pots

dangling like weird copper bats
over restaurant-grade appliances.

The second is sold at Toys R Us.
Made mostly of bright plastic,

electronic features enhance
its realism, like a microwave

that beeps when the grenade-
shaped ear of corn is cooked.

The third one is invisible.
It exists in your head,

ill-defined, unattached
to any rooms or house.

No fire or family is found in it.
The cupboards are generally bare.

But each morning, first thing,
and sometimes in the middle of the night,

you find yourself there—shivering
over the stove, whispering

to its gods, waiting
for that empty kettle to cry.

THE GRASS

I wanted something to say about the grass
but, as there was no grass, I said instead
most days are bad, especially this one,
spent mostly at the corner Laundromat,
vending machines stocked with little boxes
of Cheer, All, Bold, Snuggle, Tide, Era, Gain.

I wanted a new thought, or an old thought
in new way, or if not a thought then at least
the good feeling that a thought would arrive.
I wanted my thought to be about the grass
but, as there still was no grass, there was nothing
for my nonexistent thought to be about.

I wondered what the other people felt,
whether they wanted to think about the grass.
Our stains are not grass, not even on the knees.
When we kneel to pray, it is not on grass.
When we fall, we fall on asphalt or glass.
The stains are mostly black tar and blood.

I tried to imagine what grass would be like
if only there were some grass. Would it be a child?
A handkerchief of the Lord? The beautiful hair
of an uncut grave? I'd snuggle with the grass,
gain cheer from all grass, be bold in the tide
and era of grass—the grass my arm & hammer.

SONNET TO MYSELF

I collect rubber bands, call my sister
when I can, rinse and recycle Ziploc bags,
keep the thermostat set at sixty-five.

I mouth the words of popular songs,
drum with my thumbs the hybrid's wheel.
My dreams are about lost teeth and exams.

I will not burst upon the scene or streak
across the sky. I will never wow or thrill.
I will not become a god or an angel.

When I was a boy, I lay down in the grass
and saw in the clouds not clowns or spittoons,
not dragons on the waves of an upside down sea—

only this and this and this and this.
When gone, I will not be missed.

WHAT'S IN THE STEAMER TRUNK?

From my tummy flew three ghosts—
charcoal, umber, midnight blue,
plus a balloon-like little red one
from a coffee cup near the radio.

I was small and did not know
their names, or of finding nothing
at Aboutness Bluff but clues, remains:
tattered shirt, shoes—a compass? Ha ha.

I liked the little red one's blah blah
best till *pop!* The rest hung around
scarily, like bats, but one by one
did speak to me eventually.

Those yellow pads prove it, see?
Data stacks, hives, volcanoes sleeping—
you pick. On second thought, better not.
Hey, what's on TV?

Quiet, ghosts. Lie down with me
in front of morning chatter shows.
We'll learn how to crack and cook
an egg & that does it for the day.

Dusk, on the stoop, sauced with my
cigar, I'll send you all packing
in puffs of smoke. Farewell, ghosts,
farewell. I'll leave the lava lamp on.

YOU BET YOUR LIFE

I am the secondary duck, the duck in waiting,
understudy to the primary duck. Primary duck
dangles from a wire, bill stuffed with a hundred
bucks, a secret word stuck to his head. Meanwhile
I'm parked in a box, permanently on call, praying
for the day when primary duck gets fucked up
by a vicious uppercut from Joe Louis, crushed
under Liberace's bling, nailed by a Drysdale pitch.
Then it'll be me, not him, descending from heaven
with a Benjamin in my beak. It's just dumb luck
that he's the primary duck. I'm his doppelganger,
duplicate, identical twin. Yet there he is, hogging
the limelight, pretending I don't even exist.

Maybe you don't get where I'm going with this.
And who is this "I" now intruding to address you?
Is it secondary duck, primary duck, or is it O.M.?
Perhaps they're all aspects of a unified thing, a trinity
of two ducks and me. How cool would it be to be
duck-duck-man, money in your mouth, secret word
shining from your forehead? The only part that sucks
would be if secondary duck, tragically jealous of his
primary duck, were ignorant of his third and human self.
Put that way, I'm pretty sure he's me. Which means
it's time I recognized the cash between my teeth.
So fetch me that mirror. Let me learn my secret word.

VISITA INESPERADA

Unbidden, pink winged, she arrives
alone in her gilded boat, come down
from her tower above the town,
her heart a great pulley to the moon.

Hexagonal room, green with walls,
we sit—she upright, clasping that hand
of mine, me upside down in my head,
bone white tablecloth map of unmapped.

She summons the stuff of my world:
orange cat, blue tree, black sky, three
ways to pray, an occasional daughter,
topaz bottles of aging maybe hope.

I wish more for life than this she knows
and starts my hand across the cloth,
her sun somehow a smidgen in my palm,
rising from nothing to syllable to song.

Night is gone. Pink wings fold, cold anchor
hoists, the moon reels in its mind. Birds
bring up the dawn. Schoolchildren gather
for the pumpkin bus, a huddle of ghosts in fog.

UROBOROS

There's a thing he desires to make and be, stripped
of artifice, conceit, the urge to please, something

he knows not what, other than it's not anything
he's been or made thus far. Sometimes it seems

the way to reach it is to sit, Siddhartha-like, refusing
to speak, since words can be the most formidable

obstacle. But then he tells himself that this, too,
is nothing but appearance, a pose, that the thing

in itself is not to be confused with any teaching
or mode of being. Then he remembers there is

no thing in itself, only appearance, that this is
the foundation of whatever it is he seeks. Then

he reminds himself not to seek, but simply allow
whatever it is to be—that the moment is a poem,

that he does not have to write it. Yet there he is,
gnawing his own tail, ignoring the moon for this.

VI

ALL SAINTS' EVE

Head a bee-buzzing stump, song
a cosmic background pulse, I lived
on pills and milk with thee in me.

From a La-Z-Boy abandoned
on the basketball court, I watched
you light up the KFC, part traffic

for the rush-hour ambulance, raise
weeds from asphalt cracks, cause rain
to come down like Adidas on me,

mofo of infinite faith. Trees
were your fingers, not prints or clues.
Never were you uppercase with me.

I've missed you since. Now balding
with back fat and ring of keys, I nibble
Mint Milanos over the kitchen sink,

spy on neighbors across the street,
daughter a bunch of grapes, purple
balloons stapled to her leotard.

She steps into the night, clutching
an empty pillowcase. Iron Man is first
to pop a balloon. Next is Gandalf,

though he said he didn't mean to.
A girl without friends is just a stem
of shriveled skins by the end.

You were out there somewhere,
but you didn't care. I searched
heaven for your face, found

only the moon. By dawn, it was clear
you'd been out all night—papering
yards, smashing pumpkins, drunk

and dressed up as God knows what.

MIDDLEMARCH

The hills are still a brownish grey
but down here in town inflated elves
have given way to inflated rabbits
clutching inflated carrots.

From a window of the diner
across the street, I watch a man spit
and hitch up his pants as he crosses
the AutoZone parking lot.

The waitress refills my cup, asks
if I'm still working on that omelet.
What I'm working on is a theory
of the meaning of this life.

So far, it's just a grocery list:
bacon, bread, milk. I rack my brain
for other things, but nothing
comes to mind. It's time

to settle up. I tuck a ten
under the shaker, then remember
Lot's wife. I make sure to leave
without looking back,

but the truck is white with salt.
Weeks from now, in a patch
of pale grass, my son will hunt
for Easter eggs. The number

determines the prize. Last year
he won a chocolate bunny.
He bit off the head and peeked inside,
then wept when he saw it was hollow.

DE ANIMA

Cliff and I were lifeguards at the city pool.
One morning, as we got ready to open up,
I found a dead rabbit floating in the deep end.
Cliff came over and took a long look. He said
the rabbit was his soul. I didn't know whether
people had souls or, if we did, whether Cliff's
was that dead rabbit. All I knew is one of us
had to get it out of there before we opened.
Cliff said he couldn't do it, so that meant me.
I scooped it up with a skimmer net, bagged it,
then tossed it in the parking lot dumpster.
When I got back to poolside, I asked Cliff
how he felt about the fact that his soul was
now in a dumpster. He said it wasn't—said
it was in the water, where it always had been
and always would be. So I said, "That rabbit
is in the dumpster. If your soul is the rabbit,
then it's in there too." Cliff said, "I guess you
don't know much about souls, then, do you?"
"Guess not," I said. We tested our whistles.
Then we opened the gates and let everyone in.

AN ARGUMENT FROM THE *PHAEDO*

Flanked by corn, my truck
a rusted-out comet, tail rising
from the orange dust, music

on the radio me and mine—
but down the road it won't be.
Which raises the question:

how many times can a man
be reborn? Cebes, friend
of Socrates, said the soul

is like a coat—durable
but not everlasting, worn out
by repeated incarnations.

That would make us kin
to these ears, golden meat
wrapped in tufted husks,

the soul outside, not in,
metaphysical skin, unseen
yet tougher than matter.

Just not eternal. I'm okay
with that. Months from now,
the flesh long gone, shreds

of blackened husk will cling
to the stubble—waiting out winter,
outlasting the farmer, longing

for the great plowing under.

A BRIEF HISTORY OF THE UNIVERSE

At first, against an empty field, we appeared as random marks.
Gradually we became blobs, grew hair, eyes, and spidery legs.
We discovered clothes: triangles for women, rectangles for men.
Our bodies and lives became more complex. We found homes,
pets, and automobiles, posed stiffly under a spiked yellow sun.
Trees evolved from lollipops to trunks with crowns of limbs.
When clouds rolled in, precipitation fell in the form of Morse code:
rain the dashes, snow the dots. Snowmen were three-circle stacks.
No matter the weather, the sky was home to exactly five birds.
One evening, we found the world enclosed by a big silver circle.
We asked our daughter what it meant. She said that it was God,
then requested mac and cheese, the kind with a packet of powder
in the box. We ate it together at the kitchen table—milk in her cup,
cheap wine for us, the cosmos dangling from a magnet on the fridge.

PORTRAIT OF LEUCIPPUS

He senses somewhere the gathering
of crows, the failing of candles, the fresh
black tracks of a grim, mythic wolf.
Beneath his feet floors rot, the door
hangs unhinged. The pump is rusted stuck.

He works, hunched over an oiled block,
disassembling things—failed engines, watches
from a distant century, the chest of a limbless
motorized doll. He catalogues the gears, hangs
pistons from hooks, degreases miles of chain.

Nothing is assembled, nothing ever built.
Our machines are wrong, but the parts, he feels,
are right. And so in a thousand labeled drawers
he stores the innocent innards of things—atoms,
it seems, for the fashioner of the world to come.

EXPULSION FROM THE GARDEN OF EDEN

We paid good money for this carnival
ride but what we got was a crater full
of skulls, she groans, her red balloon
thumping in its cage of borrowed ribs.
Now, now, he whispers to her, it's not like
we lined up for the great chain of being,
but then he shuts up to suck on his inhaler
and sort of forgets what he was talking about.
She slouches off for another candied apple
at the end of a dirt path paved with snow
cone cups and corndog sticks. He lets her go
like he values her autonomy, but really
he just wants to play Whac-A-Mole alone.
Later on they exit the park together,
holding hands, ashamed, but united against
the sudden night. Old Jeb surveys all this
from a rusty gondola, stuck at the zenith
of the empyrean Ferris wheel. He sighs
and slumps behind a clump of cotton candy
so humongous you'd mistake it for a cloud.

A THURSDAY IN AND ABOVE THE WORLD

Seen in the right light, the light
of morning in October, the toast
on your plate smiles up at you.

Later, when the light is right
for other things, you spot gods
in the clouds above Burger King.

You wait in traffic for the light
to turn green, you and millions more
on a mission to Home Depot.

There the light is different, divine
in its own way, ineffable, detectable
only with the aid of certain pills,

pink and round, through which
the plumbing aisle becomes a place
where grace of a suburban sort

descends and makes quick friends
of strangers. You see the saffron robe
in your helper's orange apron.

As for this Fluidmaster fill valve,
could anything be more sublime?
The sun now shines on everyone.

Back home, all alone, you repair
the upstairs toilet. The kids won't notice
a thing. Your labor and love are lost

on them, but the universe takes note.
Or so to you it seems, its spiral rings
reflected in the water as it wheels.

BOOK OF JOHN

John is on all fours in the gravel.
Ask him and he's a lamb, grazing
on the moon, waiting for the bus

to school. On a nearby bench,
she studies John, highlights passages
in pink, wonders what word

was in the beginning, why word
became flesh, which words were her
beginning, what words became John.

The angel cloaked her in his gin-soaked
wings and said unto her, Am I hurting you?
Do you want me to stop?

Before those words was flesh,
in flesh the life, in life the love
and savagery of men. She died

back then but doesn't know
if it was for or from his sins.
The bus pulls up. She shepherds

her son to the stop. Behold! The lamb
of John ascending from the moon,
now bound for the light

and the darkness of the world.

A BRIEF SYNOPSIS OF SPINOZA'S *ETHICS*

The sound of his sister's laugh fills the cove.
Her children tumble from the sky like fruit,
vanish, rise from the churn, return to the dock
to do a cannonball, jackknife, or flying squirrel.
He sits in the shade, snaps pics with his phone,
a Pittsburgh Steelers sleeve hugging his beer.

God is everywhere if anywhere, but right here
especially—or so he nearly believes, if only
in the moment before arguments rush in,
reminding him the world makes zero sense
if created and governed by a perfect being.

Let the being be imperfect, then. Let it be
this beer, this family, this olive-colored lake.
Let it be the boat that brought us here, the vanity
of all our striving, the shocking sight of blood
in urine, the sickness that will finally do us in.
Let it be, till then, the now of her laughter
as from heaven her children fall one by one.

CAROUSEL

(a mirrorform)

We feel ourselves falling out of something again
and into something other, but neither thing
is known, and this cycle of falling in and out of
unknowns is itself a something we know not what.
We scan the horizons, squint into books, pray
to the unknown knower of all things for a way
to comprehend the shed skin, the crimson cut,
the grander scheme whose end we hope is love—
or if not to comprehend, then at least to sing
in tune with the becoming that has always been.

THE SAME BARE PLACE

(a *mirrorform*)

When, too late for remedy, your life amounts
to nothing, when the lists you made are good
for nothing, when the nothing you are stares
nothingness in the face, focus on something
particular—glass on the asphalt, a mailbox,
a bowl, a lizard sunning on the river rocks,
and from there build outward, ring upon ring,
yourself underneath, the shoulder that bears
the whole world up. Shrug then, if you would—
but know, below the nothing, the thing that counts.

NOTES

"Jake's Ladder": In *Genesis* 28:10–17, Jacob dreams of a ladder that reaches heaven.

"Twelve Pzalms to Our Lord Bubba": A woefully inadequate homage to John Berryman's masterpiece, *The Dream Songs*.

"The Republic": This poem is indebted to the Theory of Forms presented in Plato's *Republic*, especially in Book VII's famous Allegory of the Cave.

"Triceratops ♥ You": The final stanzas allude to a scene in the film *Jurassic Park* (1993), directed by Steven Spielberg, in which scientists played by Laura Dern and Sam Neill come to the aid of an ailing triceratops.

"Northeast Kingdom": Lines 1–4 of the second stanza make use of imagery from the paintings of Dorian Vallejo, particularly *Small Windows* and *Nighttime Sea Journey*.

"Thong Man": Lines 11–12 point to poems by T. S. Eliot, Robert Frost, and Wallace Stevens.

"Crossing the Water": The first three lines of the sixth stanza quote from Sylvia Plath's poem of the same title.

"Visita Inesperada": This poem is informed by imagery from Remedios Varo Uranga's painting of the same title (1958), as well as her *Exploración de las fuentes del río Orinoco* (1959).

"Report from the Surface": I read somewhere that the poet Anne Carson, whose work I admire, was for a time obsessed with painting volcanoes.

"The Grass": The final stanza contains fragments of lines from Walt Whitman's "Song of Myself."

"You Bet Your Life": This poem exploits elements of Groucho Marx's quiz show, *You Bet Your Life*, which ran on NBC-TV from 1950 to 1961.

"Middlemarch": The title comes from George Eliot's novel, which—importantly for this poem—is subtitled "A Study of Provincial Life."

"De Anima": The title of Aristotle's treatise on souls.

"An Argument from the *Phaedo*": In that dialogue, Socrates, just moments away from death, argues that the soul is immortal; his friends, including Cebes, are not so sure.

"Portrait of Leucippus": After the fifth century (BCE) founder of the philosophy of atomism.

"Book of John": Lines in this poem echo verses from the *Gospel of John*.

"A Brief Synopsis of Spinoza's *Ethics*": In the *Ethics* (1677), Spinoza defends a form of pantheism.

"The Same Bare Place": The title comes from a line in "The Snow Man" by Wallace Stevens.

ACKNOWLEDGMENTS

I'm grateful to the editors of the following journals in which versions of these poems first appeared:

32 Poems, "Compressed Sponge"
American Literary Review, "In the U-Haul Parking Lot" and "Sonnet for a Changed Climate"
Boulevard, "Dream Kitchen" and "Triceratops ♥ You"
Bellevue Literary Review, "Adelia"
Boaat, "What's in the Steamer Trunk?"
Carolina Quarterly, "Report from the Surface" and "Visita Inesperada"
Chattahoochee Review, "Crossing the Water"
Columbia Poetry Review, "In the Car on the Way to My Girlfriend's Brother's Funeral"
The Cossack Review, "An Argument from the *Phaedo*"
Field, "Mother Tongue"
Fugue, "Click Here to Get Ripped"
Hayden's Ferry Review, "De Anima," "Rocket Man," and "SOS Pad"
Lake Effect, "Flood"
The Massachusetts Review, "Igloo"
The Minnesota Review, "In My Wife's Vegetable Garden"
The Missouri Review, "A Brief History of the Universe"
The Moth, "Sonnet to Myself"
New England Review, "Uroboros"
Passages North, "La Fin de L'ete"
The Pinch, "Body Image," "Here's the Thing," "Shop-Rite," "Someone Just Searched for You," and "Thong Man"
Pleiades, "A Brief Synopsis of Spinoza's Ethics" and "A Thursday In and Above the World"
Ploughshares, "Mementomori.com"
Poetry Northwest, "All Saints' Eve" and "Expulsion from the Garden of Eden"
Radar Poetry, "Northeast Kingdom"

Raintown Review, "Still Life"

River Styx, "Middlemarch"

Salamander, "Rivers"

Southeast Review, "You Bet Your Life"

Southern Poetry Review, "Cumulus Mediocris"

The Southern Review, "Black Ring" and "The Saddest Poem in Pennsylvania"

Spillway, "Book of John"

Sugar House Review, "Beam," "Lethe," and "Portrait of Leucippus"

Sycamore Review, "The Grass"

Tahoma Literary Review, "Twelve Pzalms to Our Lord Bubba"

Thrush Poetry Journal, "The Republic"

Willow Springs, "Grief"

The Yale Review, "Something You Left to Me"

Thanks also to the editors of Poetry Daily for republishing "Rocket Man" and "Something You Left to Me," which first appeared in *Hayden's Ferry Review* and *The Yale Review*, respectively, and to the editors of Verse Daily for republishing "Triceratops ♥ You," originally published in *Boulevard*.

So much is determined by luck, and I was extraordinarily lucky to have this manuscript fall into the hands of two people to whom I'm profoundly indebted: Rosanna Warren, who selected it as the winner of the 2018 Vassar Miller Prize in Poetry, and John Poch, editor of the Vassar Miller series. I'd also like to thank two fine people at UNT Press: Karen DeVinney, for turning my manuscript into this book, and Bess Whitby, for getting it into the hands of readers.

In the fall of 2014, when I began to get serious about poetry, Lee Upton graciously allowed me to audit her undergraduate course in the history of modern and contemporary poetry. Lee was a superabundant source of wisdom, kindness, and encouragement during that semester, and has been so ever since. I'm grateful to her for all of it.

I'm grateful to many other people who supported my work in one way or another. I think especially of Rob Blunt, Paul Cefalu, Ben and Chris Cohen, Fred Feldman, Margaret Leef, Alix Ohlin, and George Panichas. I beg the forgiveness of anyone whose name should be mentioned here, but isn't.

My remaining debts are too deep to be fathomed. These are to my parents, Mary Adelia McLeod and Mac McLeod, and to my partner, Lijuan Xu. Without those three, neither these poems nor the poet would be.

CPSIA information can be obtained
at www.ICGtesting.com
Printed in the USA
BVHW080815060219
539571BV00003B/44/P

9 781574 417494